LISTEN

WISDOM AND WIT FOR THE NEXT GENERATIONS

WAYNE S. BROWN

To Lee,
Thank You for taking
the time to ... LISTEN

THANK YOU

I want to thank God for being kind and merciful towards me, and giving me life. To my lovely wife Laura, every day with you is sweeter than the day before. To my children, Ouidaintria, Aurelius, and LaTasha, you are my hope for the future. To my granddaughters, Serenity and Harmony, your names are your destiny. To my grandson Justice, every day is a Sonny day. To my parents Irenus and Inez, without you there would be no Wayne. To my siblings, Ralph and Diane, you've always loved and supported your baby brother. To David and Sylvia Banks, your leadership and friendship is inspirational. To my SWAT comrades, we did it! To my team of editors, much love. To TaShauna, I love you. To all my relatives and friends, thank you for your prayers and your encouragement.

WAYNE S. BROWN

CONTENTS

INTRODUCTION

When I was growing up, I loved family get-togethers, especially those that didn't include a funeral. I saw relatives that I hadn't seen for quite some time. It was usually a time filled with joy, laughter, and sharing. The elders of the family would sometimes sit on the porch and share their wisdom about life, relationships, health, and faith. Some of us would listen while others respectfully stared off into space. As I grew older, I realized that if I would have applied half of the advice I received, I would have avoided many failures, heartbreaks, and financial losses. Wisdom and knowledge from those who had "been there, done that" was priceless. I also understand that those nuggets of wisdom and knowledge should be preserved and given to the next generation, not only orally, but also in the written word. The purpose of this book is to pass along some of those precious nuggets that were given to me my by the sages.

The book is divided into four sections: Spiritual, Physical, Emotional, and Financial. At the end of each chapter, there is a summary of the main points in the section called "Did You Hear What I Said". This section is dedicated to those whose minds wandered while the elders were talking. As you read these gems, I hope that this book spurs you to think critically, laugh occasionally, and love unconditionally.

SPIRITUAL

WAYNE S. BROWN

MAKE JESUS YOUR LORD

As far back as I can remember, I was always in church. Our family attended a church on Lincoln Ave in Albany, GA. It was a small church with wooden slat pews that gave very little back support and no comfort to the parishioner. I still remember Sister Horton teaching our Sunday School class.

One of my favorite songs was:

I shall not be
I shall not be moved
I shall not be
I shall not be moved
Just like a tree
That's planted by the water
I shall not be moved[1]

Once Sunday School was over at 11:00, we had a 15 minute break until Morning Worship. The order of worship was: Opening Prayer, two songs, Scripture, Main Prayer, two songs, Preaching, Invitation, Communion, Offering, Announcements, and Closing Prayer. All in all, the service lasted for about an hour.

I was a fidgety child, and after about 20 minutes I would start moving and talking, which didn't sit well with my parents. Momma was a master at ninja-type smacks. These blows came out of nowhere and with extreme accuracy. Daddy was a different story. He would give a stern look. One would think that was enough for a young boy. After all, I lived with him so I knew what was next.....kind of. He would curl

---

[1] Author unknown.

his middle finger into his thumb and unleashed "The Thump". This would hurt, but it bought the least attention from everyone. The trip outside was what made everyone look. I could see my friends' faces as we proceeded past the sanctuary. The word bubbles above their heads said, "Dead Man Walking".

Once outside, everything was a blur. I do remember that it was quick and my clothes were disheveled when I regained my bearings. After that, I was good for another 20 minutes and service was almost over. This wasn't an every Sunday occurrence. To be truthful, most of my memories of Lincoln Ave. were good. Life was very simple.

When I was eight, the congregation moved into a larger building on River Road. Everyone in the congregation was excited. My friend Keith and I were in the picture of the ribbon cutting ceremony. The memories of River Road were just as special as the memories of Lincoln Ave. I received so much love and support that I never experienced loneliness, abandonment, or rejection. I was truly blessed to have such a caring extended family. In school, I always had someone watching out for me. After school I couldn't go anywhere without one of the members of the church

> **Momma was a quiet prayer warrior**

being somewhere in the area. Little did I know many of my peers did not have the same support. Thank God for my extended family.

At home, God was the center of our lives. Daddy and Momma didn't leave their faith at the church. They brought it home and showed us that faith was a lifestyle. Momma was the quiet prayer warrior. She reminds me of Hannah in the book of Samuel. When Hannah prayed, her lips moved but her words were not audible. Even though other people couldn't hear what Momma was saying, I could hear every word. I could hear her asking God to watch over me, and Heaven knows I needed it.

Daddy was more outspoken. His prayers would begin with:

> *"Father we come to thee in the hour of prayer*
> *Thanking thee for the many rich blessings*
> *thou has richly bestowed upon us*
> *From the earliest existences of our lives*
> *down to this present time…"*

I always wondered where he learned how to pray. When he prayed it seemed like everything would stop to hear what he was saying. It was as if he were in the courtroom making his closing arguments to the judge. Perhaps he missed his calling. Nevertheless, his prayers were moving. When I was a teenager he took me to a church he attended when he was young. The church seemed like it was caught in an ante-bellum time warp. It was a white edifice with wooden floors. The ceilings had a high pitch. There were a few lights, each hung from a single wire that extended from the high point in the ceiling. In one of the lights there was a wasp nest that had a drone hovering it. I believe the pews were the same pews from Lincoln Ave.

Some women at the church were dressed in white. I kept wondering why the church needed so many nurses[2]. The ladies began to sing a song that I did not recognize; however, the song was very moving. While they were singing, they kept a steady cadence with their feet striking the floor like a bass drum. While sitting and listening, I noticed that I felt something stirring

---

[2] At the church, the ushers wore white dresses that resembled a nurses uniform

within me. It was the same feeling I had when Daddy prayed. When the women finished singing, a deacon came to the front to lead prayer. As soon as he began I knew this was the place Daddy had learned to pray. I hoped I would be able to pray like that. I wanted to be able to speak and people be moved. I wanted to be imbued with the ability to go before the throne of God and speak on behalf of others. That was my sincere prayer.

My grandmother, Ma Gussie, was also a person of prayer. On Fridays I would spend the night with her. On Saturday mornings, she would get up and fix breakfast which consisted of Cream of Wheat, toast, and eggs. Before we could eat, she would reach for the small ceramic loaf of bread which contained individual strips of paper. Each strip contained a bible verse. She would read the bible verse and place the strip back in the loaf. Then she would pray. Her lips would move and the words were almost inaudible….just like Momma. Ma Gussie also prayed that God would watch over me and He honored her request. I was surrounded by so much prayer and so much power that being successful should have been a breeze. However, instead of following the path of prayer, I wanted to forge my own path and be my own person.

I enlisted in the US Air Force two months after graduating from high school. I thought I was grown. I could do what I wanted, when I wanted, and there was no one from River Road that would go back and tell on me. This new-found freedom came with choices. On Sunday I could go to church or not. I could eat and not thank God for the food. In fact, I could go all week and not acknowledge that God, Jesus, or the Holy Spirit even existed (this is the part where God honored their prayers and watched over me in spite of myself). As time moved on, I became more distant from God and life began to kick in high gear.

Trying to be grown, I found out soon enough that I couldn't find my butt with both hands. When I was 20, I was married with a child on the way, now responsible for two other people besides myself. At 22, my wife, Pam, was pregnant with our second child and I still couldn't find my butt. At 23, we separated for the first time. One reason for the breakup was that I

> *I became more distant from God*

found my butt...then I lost my head. Several bad decisions had strained the marriage and nearly derailed my career. Fortunately, the Air Force needed me in Sicily. I thought that this would be a new beginning. I would leave the old people, places, and habits, and get a fresh start on life. However, that would not be the case.

The new location seemed to be going well. I talked with Pam and we decided to give love a try...again. She and the kids came to Sicily. Within a couple of weeks she noticed that some of those bad habits followed me to our new abode, which led to more bad decisions and more arguing. My family left Sicily after a few months. Their stay was so short that when the movers came they noticed that several boxes had not been unpacked since they dropped them off a few months earlier (this should have been a sign). I stayed in Sicily for another year and a half before being assigned to Beale Air Force Base, CA.

Pam and I decided to give love a third try. Within a couple of months of our arrival, the verdict was in and we knew that it was time to part ways. The divorce was amicable. We decided that the kids would be with me. Yet, this left me more frightened than when I first became a father. This time around, I found myself trying to fall back on the prayers of Momma, Daddy, and Ma Gussie. I tried to sing the old songs that I remembered from church. I even started quoting scriptures that I hadn't let come out of my mouth in years. Nothing seemed to work. I continued to try to duplicate the faith I had as a young boy; but I wasn't that young boy anymore.

I began to acknowledge the fact that I needed a relationship with God, and that's when my life began to change. Instead of going back to River Road or Lincoln Ave, I went back to God. I realized that there was more to Him than going to church. It was more than saying a prayer and more than giving an offering. I also found that it wasn't super deep spiritual event. It was simple and similar to the relationship I have with my parents and loved ones. Just as I show my love for them it starts on the inside. I shouldn't have to go around with a sign that says "I love my parents" or "I love my wife". Anyone that sees how we interact with each other will know I love them. So my love for God started from within and manifested itself through my actions.

Managing my family, finances, and career became easier. A little over a year after the divorce, I met Laura. She was a single mom with a five year old daughter. We were married and did our version of the Brady Bunch[3]. We've been together for over 22 years and Jesus has been and is the center of our marriage. We have our personal relationships with Jesus and we have our relationship with Jesus as a couple. Now I can tell you I've learned that Jesus has to be at the center of your life. Many people have done great things and give God zero credit for anything. If that is how you want to live your life, then that's a choice you have to make. As for me and my house, we choose to serve the Lord. Now that I've made that choice, I can truly sing, "I shall not be moved".

_____

[3] The Brady Bunch were a 70's television family where a single father with three sons married a single mother with three daughters.

Did You Hear What I Said?

1. Is your relationship with God based on what you believe or is it based on what you remember?
2. List the priorities in your life. What position is Jesus on your list?
3. Each choice in life has either good or bad consequences, so take ownership of the choices you make.

WAYNE S. BROWN

Why Am I Here?

At some point in life many people have asked themselves this question. I haven't talked to many five-year-olds that concern themselves with this question. However, in the tweens and teen years the question causes concern. During this time kids are trying to find their personal identity in the midst of trying to fit in with their peers. Along with trying to find their identity, they are also trying to adjust to their emotional growth. They are told that they need to "grow up" and "stop being such a baby". Fortunately, my family supported me and let me know that this time would pass and that I would be okay. In spite of their encouragement I still had times when I wondered "why I am here?"

Like my peers, I had dreams of what I wanted to be when I grew up. Once I wanted to be a truck driver like my Daddy. Then he became a carpenter and I knew I did not want to follow his footsteps in that career. I decided that I wanted to be a DJ, but I was too frugal (okay cheap) to purchase all the latest music. Next, I wanted to be a preacher; the hooping type. I loved how the preacher's voice would modulate and how he could tell a story and make people feel that they were in the middle of an exciting event. However, when I saw how the preacher's life was always under a microscope, I figured I should go back to sleep and come up with another dream.

According to Merriam-Webster, one of the definitions of a dream is "a condition or achievement that is longed for; an aspiration; a wild fancy or hope" (Merriam-Webster). These dreams are not the ones that come from eating old collard greens or watching a movie that makes you turn on every light in the house prior to going to bed. The dreams that I am referring to are dreams that take you beyond your present situation and give you a glimpse of what you can achieve. It is interesting to note that dreams are not tainted by reality. Because of their present situations, some people have stopped dreaming and accepted their status in life. They live in a self-imposed caste system where death is the only way out. This is a bleak and hopeless existence.

The book of Genesis gives us an account of Joseph and his interaction with his brothers. Joseph was definitely a dreamer whose dreams were given to him by God. His dreams went beyond his cognitive apprehension. To think that the sun, moon, and stars could bow down to him was surely beyond his wildest dreams. It also went beyond his family's wildest dreams. His siblings developed animosity towards Joseph and plotted to kill him. Instead of murder, they sold him into slavery. Joseph went from slavery to prison where he was mistreated and forgotten, yet he never stopped

> **Dreams are not tainted by reality**

being a dreamer. Finally, he got his chance to be released from prison. All he had to do was to interpret the king's dream. God gave him the interpretation and Joseph instantly went from the prison to the palace. What would have happened had he stopped being a dreamer?

What would have happened if Dr. Martin Luther King, Jr. would have stopped dreaming? Here are some of the words to his famous speech:

"I say to you today, my friends, so even though we face the difficulties of today and tomorrow, I still have a dream.
It is a dream deeply rooted in the American dream.
I have a dream that one day this nation will rise up and live out the true meaning of its creed:
"We hold these truths to be self-evident: that all men are created equal." (US Constitution)

How many times must he have wanted to give up on his dream? How many moments of doubt flooded his mind as he sat in a putrid Birmingham jail cell? Yet he continued to persevere. As with Joseph, Dr. King knew that his dream was not only for his benefit, but for the benefit of generations to come. This speech was delivered in 1963 and in 2014 we continue to reap the benefits of that dream.

My grandfather, Henry Brown Sr. had a dream. He wanted to give each of his children their own land to farm. This was a tall order considering the fact that he had 15 children. He did not let his current situation prevent him from dreaming. As a black man in Early County, GA in the early 1900's, I would dare say that the odds were stacked against him being able to carry out his dream. Nevertheless, he worked as hard as he could to make the dream come true. He accumulated several hundred acres of land. As time has passed, the land deed exchanged hands several times. However, I am proud to say that some of the land is still owned by family members. So yes, the family is benefiting from the dreams of a dreamer.

From dreams we move into plans. Plans are "a set of actions that have been thought of as a way to do or achieve something." (Merriam-Webster) When I was graduating from high school my plan was to go into the Air Force. Daddy had a different plan for me. His plan was for me to go to college and earn my degree. This was a good plan, but it wasn't my plan. For several months this difference of opinion was "the elephant in the room". He let me know his displeasure through his silence and I remained steadfast, unmovable, and continued to abound in my own way of thinking. My plans were geared toward the Air Force. While I didn't listen to Daddy's plan, I also did not listen to my Heavenly Father's plan. In fact, I did not ask Him for His plan for me because it may have interfered with my plans. When I think about it now, I have to say that my thought process was profoundly asinine (and that's putting it mildly). The Creator of Heaven and Earth had a perfect plan for my life and I said, "No thank you, I've got a better plan." A paraphrase of Robert Burns' poem "To a Mouse" says,

"The best laid schemes (plans) of mice and men go often awry" (MacLachlan)

Fortunately, God allowed me to follow through with my plan and I was able to have a successful 30-year career. Here's something to think about, what would have happened if I would have asked God about His plan for my life? He may have responded, "Go, and I'll be with you every step of the way." I am glad that God spared me and allowed me to align myself with His plan and His purpose.

Purpose is defined as "the reason why something is done or used; the aim or intention of something." (Merriam-Webster) In other words, "What is my purpose?" Prior to anything being made, the purpose is already determined.

An example would be a carpenter building a house. The first question that the carpenter asks is "What is the purpose of the house?" "Who will live in the house?" These questions must be answered prior to any walls being erected. Even mosquitoes and roaches have a purpose and I hope they know it, because I have no idea what it is. You can see that everything has a purpose. Also, everyone has a purpose.

You were designed with purpose in mind. This purpose has been embedded into your DNA. Prior to your birth and prior to your parents meeting each other, there was a specific purpose for your existence. Without purpose, life has little or no meaning. Some people have worked several decades to amass large sums of money, only to find out that there is something still missing. They develop a "bucket list" and when they finish the last item on the list, they continue to feel unsatisfied. Some people try extreme sports. The thought is if I push myself beyond my limits, I can achieve some type of nirvana.

Todd Marinovich was a superstar in

Everything has a purpose...even mosquitoes

football. As a high school graduate, he was the number one recruit in the nation. He made the cover of ESPN Magazine and was given the name, Robo-Kid. When he went to college his career took off. He was on the national stage and he flourished until drugs and alcohol began to take control. His game began to decline, but, his skills were so exceptional that his B game was better than everyone's A game. He was drafted into the NFL and his future looked bright. However, instead of breaking records he ended up as an addict and eventually left the NFL. The great news is that he recovered and is helping others.   During an interview, what resonated with e was when he said, "Just because someone is good at something doesn't mean that's what they are supposed to do for the rest of their life." (ESPN) Being good at something should not outweigh pursuing your purpose.

You may be asking, "How do I pursue my purpose when I don't know what it is?" You may have already experienced someone telling you your purpose. When they finished, you may or may not have agreed with them. What if you could find your purpose without someone else telling you your purpose? Dr. David Banks developed a Purpose Discovery Worksheet. It is a simple form that helps you to answer this question for yourself. Here is my purpose statement that I developed:

"To motivate and encourage people in discovering and using their unique gifts. Challenging them to be more than just average, thus enabling them to live a life of impact and fulfillment."

Everything I do has to align with my purpose. If a something doesn't line up with my purpose, then I count it as a fun activity that is only for a short period of time. Think of all the time you could save by not following after things that do not align with your purpose. Many of us could have avoided changing our college major during our junior year. Some of us would not have taken jobs just because it paid "good money". Please learn from our mistakes and make the most of life.

Did You Hear What I Said?

1. Go www.bridgenthegap.com and click the "PURPOSE" tab to sign up for your personal Purpose Discovery session.
2. Fulfillment is intentional and must be pursued. Make a plan on how to fulfill your purpose
3. While in pursuit of purpose, make sure you have some fun along the way.

Know Who You Are in God

During a job interview, you may be asked to tell a little about yourself. Your pitch may start with your name, occupation, skills, and years of experience. Casual introductions are normally similar: name, marital status, number of children, and hobbies. Depending on the situation, the introduction may vary. Some people identify themselves by their family ties. At the family reunions I am known as, Buck's son, Nez' baby, and I've even been called

"Ralph" (my brother who is nine years older and six inches taller).

Family lineage is important, or at least it should be. During our family reunion in 2008, everyone received a booklet about our family. I could begin with Daddy, who was the son of Henry, who was the son of Cornelia, who was the daughter of Adam who was the son of a slave that came to Early County, GA with his master, Mr. Shackleford, in 1840. My maternal lineage starts with my mother, Inez, who is the daughter of Gussie Mae, (who was the daughter of Lizzie) and James Charlie (nicknamed JC), who is the son of Axie. Each name is significant because each predecessor is a part of who I am. More significantly, family lineage is only PART of my identity.

When I graduated from high school and left home, I wanted to make a name for myself. I was proud of my family name, but I wanted people to know that I AM WAYNE. After a year of being away, I came home for the weekend to visit my parents. While walking in the mall I saw a minister from River Road. We greeted each other and he asked me if I was going to a church event later that night. My reply was, "No." Then he looked at me in disbelief and said, "Are you Brother Brown's son?" In an instant I wanted to scream, "NO! I AM WAYNE!" Truth be told, back then and now, it feels good when someone asks me, "Are you Bro. Brown's son?"

In the book of Matthew, the author gives a detailed list of the lineage of Jesus. This list shows that Jesus is the son of David, whose forefather was Abraham. Jesus lineage proved that He was the promised Messiah. He was more than just an awesome teacher and a miracle worker. His pedigree proved that He was the Chosen One, Abraham's seed. There are other biblical instances where family identity was crucial. In the book of Kings, belonging to a specific family lineage could literally mean life or death. After Solomon's reign, the kingdom was split into the Northern Kingdom and Judah. The Northern Kingdom had an interesting way of transitioning between the old and new regimes. The new king would seize the throne and then try to blot out the family of the preceding king. The reason for the purging was that the new king realized that one of the descendants of the former king would defend the family name and try to retake the throne. The family name was paramount to one's identity.

The author Alex Haley spent years trying to trace his lineage back to Africa, the Motherland.

As a result of his research, the mini-series Roots was aired in 1977 and many African American wanted to find their family's "Kunta Kinte"[4] to prove they were descendants of kings and queens. Author and historian Henry Louis Gates Jr. has also extensively studied African American lineage.   His work revealed a rich African heritage and the non-romanticized side of West Africa.   He exposed how some tribes enslaved other tribes prior to being sold to slave runners. This caused much uproar in the African-American community.   No matter how we look at lineage, we can conclude that family lines (good and bad) are an important part of knowing your identity.

Tracing the ancestry to Africa was powerful for the African-American community.   It gave hope and identity to people who believed they had no value or self-worth.   We started wearing our hair differently and designing our clothes with an African influence.   Momma even made me a dashiki[5].   I was proud to wear it because I felt I was getting in touch with my African roots.

---

[4] Kunta Kinte was captured in Africa and bought to America as a slave.

[5] The dashiki was a brightly colored shirt or blouse, many were patterned after the West African garment

Not to mention that one of the girls in class said that I looked cute in my dashiki. This was also the time when "ethnic" names were popular. Names like Michael and Katherine were exchanged for Malik and Khadijah. Wayne and Pam Brown jumped on the bandwagon also. Our daughter's name is Ouidaintria Latreva (pronounced We-dain-tree-ah La-tree-vah). I didn't know what the name meant, but it was definitely unique.

I find it interesting that when tracing our lineage, we as African Americans stop at Africa. I've also noticed that other ethnic groups tend to stop at a certain point in the history. Some people of European descent might trace their lineage back to a king in England. They may have a picture of their family crest displayed in a prominent place in their home because they are proud of being direct descendants of royalty. Others may trace their lineage to Scandinavia and now see themselves as the heirs of Erik the Great.

It seems that most people that I've met want to prove they are possessors of noble heritage. This can be a positive motivator. I still have one question to ask, "Why do we stop?" Why don't we pursue tracing our heritage as far back as we can go? In the book of Luke the physician places a comma after Abraham and keeps going. He lists 20 more names and end with "....who was the son of God." If you are going to identify with a family heritage, then ending the list with "who was the son of God" places you in pretty good company. The next time you trace your lineage, make sure you trace it back to God, who is our Father.

When I talk with young people I often ask, "If you found out that you are an heir of the Hurst Family (or any wealthy family), how would that change the way you think and act?" That question would get a wide range of answers. Some would say, "I'd be the same person, just richer." Others would say, "I'd help a lot of people" or "I wouldn't tell anyone". The truth is that if you realized that you had almost unlimited access to resources, your attitude would change. Think back to the first time you received a paycheck. Your attitude immediately changed, especially if you could spend the money on what you desired. Now, try to exponentially multiply that attitude. Your thinking would not be limited to college, a job,

> **Trace your lineage back to God**

and responsibilities. You could focus on education, legacy, and philanthropic endeavors also. Well guess what? You do have access. This entrance is gained by knowing who you are in God. Israel Houghton and Chris Tomlin recorded a song entitled "I Know Who I Am". The chorus is simple:

I know who I am
I know who I am
I know who I am
I am yours
I am yours
And You are Mine
Jesus, You are Mine (Houghton)

These simple words are powerful. When you know who you are in God, you can avoid others taking advantage of you and making you who they want you to be.

I had the privilege of meeting and talking with Laura Johnston-Kohl. (Johnston-Kohl) She is now a 6th grade teacher who was an activist during the Civil Rights Movement. As a white teenager growing up in the 60's, Laura always stood up for what was right. In 1963, her mother opened up their home to travelers attending the 1963 March on Washington.

When Laura was a young adult, she protested against the Vietnam War. She was one of those Hippie/Flower children that were on the news protesting in front of the White House.

While living in New Haven CT, she opened her home to the Black Panther Party. They held regular meetings in her home. Laura was integral in providing free breakfast to children in the community. She admitted that she was a bit naïve about the seriousness of being associated with the Black Panthers. Her naivety was lost when a bullet came through her window and struck one of the Panthers. Shortly after the incident, Laura's sister stepped in to help her make sense of what was happening and the consequences of the choices she had made.

Laura moved to California with her sister. Within a few weeks after arrival, she heard about a group that was active in the community and was making a difference in people's lives. She felt she could again stand up for the underprivileged. The group was called the People's Temple and their charismatic leader was Jim Jones. He was the catalyst for change in the San Francisco area. He had formed a multicultural community that fought for justice and equality.

Laura was not a religious person; therefore, God was not the center of her decision to become a part of the People's Temple commune. She

> **For Laura, being all-in was part of her identity**

was more interested in the "cause". She worked tirelessly to help others. One of her jobs was to drive a bus. She and others would drive the fleet of Temple buses across the country to promote different projects. The drivers were so dedicated that while one person was driving, the relief driver would sleep in the luggage compartment of the bus. In this way, the buses could travel non-stop until they reached their destination. For Laura, being all-in was part of her identity and sacrificing was something that came natural to her.

As time passed, Laura was chosen to go to Jonestown, Guyana. Her job was to purchase, track, and transport supplies for supplying the new establishment. To accomplish this, she spent time in Georgetown, which was the capital city. Laura would ensure that the supplies were purchased and placed on the boat for transport. In November 1978, she was part of the welcoming committee that met Senator Leo Ryan and his delegation in Georgetown. The committee's task was to persuade the delegation that everything in Jonestown was great. Laura had no idea that after Senator Ryan left, that she would never see most of her Temple family again. While she remained in Georgetown, the delegation was murdered and over 900 People's Temple members were found dead.[6]

The memories of that fateful day will always be etched in Laura's mind. She recalled how there were signs that things were going awry, but, she ignored the signs and pressed forward for the cause. Her story made me stop and take inventory. There were times in my life where I really didn't know my identity. I knew I was concerned with helping others and I was always willing to go the extra mile to make sure the job got done. The element that I was missing was not having an identity outside of the group that I was associated with. As you can see, this line of thinking can lead to serious and deadly consequences. Know who you are in God. Your life and the lives of others may depend on it.

---

[6] To know more about Laura's story, read her book "Jonestown Survivor."

Did You Hear What I Said?

1. Your lineage is an important element in knowing your identity.
2. Your lineage does not stop at a location in another continent, it stops at Genesis, "...in the beginning God...".
3. Knowing your identity gives you confidence to stand on your own in the midst of trouble.

PHYSICAL

WAYNE S. BROWN

Take Care of Yourself

loved visiting my cousins and friends in Blakely, GA. It was an hour's drive from Albany. Upon arrival, I would jump out of the car and ask Aunt Edith for a piece of Bazooka bubble gum. Then it was time to have some fun on the baseball field and playing in the red clay. After a day of having fun I was covered with dirt and smelled like fresh-cut onions from Jimmy's Hotdogs. When I got in the car, Momma would shake her head and roll the window down to get some fresh air. As we were leaving someone would kindly say, "Take care yourself." The word "of" was usually left out of the statement. It was our way of saying that we bid you good health and hope to see you soon. As I grew up the phrase "take care yourself" began to mean more to me. It became more of a mandate than a kind regard. As the people I loved began to pass away I realized life was short, and it was shorter when you didn't take care of yourself.

From day one of Basic Military Training, physical fitness was stressed day and night. In order to complete all of the tasks required during the day, you had to be physically fit. The morning began with push-ups, sit-ups, jumping jacks, and running. I was not Forrest Gump and I did not like running. After morning calisthenics, we marched everywhere we needed to go. By the time evening came, we had logged several miles between marching, running, and walking. Prior to basic training, I was in pretty good shape. By the end of Basic, I was in better shape.

After finishing Basic Training, fitness was stressed, just not as much. Since it wasn't a priority anymore, I decided to put fitness on the back burner. Time moved on and I began to gain a little weight. Since I started Basic Training at 115 pounds, gaining a little weight

> My motto was "work hard, play harder"

wasn't really that bad. The problem was that the weight was fat and not muscle. My fitness regimen started in the early morning by waking up late and rushing to work. My first job in the Air Force was as an Administrative Assistant. I was assigned to the Base Contracts Office where I was a Keypunch Operator (this was long before personal computers) and I sorted and distributed mail. Therefore, my physical activity during the day wasn't very demanding. After work, I spent more time doing 12 ounce curls[7] than I did working out at the gym.

While stationed at Holloman AFB, NM, I was an Aerospace Ground Equipment Technician. That meant that I was a cross between a mechanic, an electrician, and a hydraulic technician. Now my work days were spent knee deep in oil, dirt, and grease instead of being behind a desk. My motto at that time was to work hard and play harder. Playing harder also meant that I still was not going to the gym to stay in shape. Also, I moved up from

---

[7] This refers to 12 ounce cans of beer

12 ounce curls to 32 ounce curls[8]. This personalized training did not aid in my preparation for the annual Air Force Fitness test which included a mile and a half run. Needless to say I barely passed the run. In fact, I think the timekeeper felt sorry for me and passed me in spite of my pathetic attempt at running.

My wake-up call came later during the first year at Holloman. My first wife and I were separated, my career was at a stand-still, and I really didn't care much about anything. One afternoon some friends invited me to a cook-out. I went to the closet to get some fresh clothes and head out to the party. This was the 80's, I put on a tank top, some shorts, white socks, tennis shoes, and sunglasses. I walked past the mirror to make sure I was looking good. I was looking, but it wasn't good. My arms had no definition. They looked like dangling dowels that connected my hands to my shoulders. My side profile wasn't any better. From the waist up my body resembled the letter "b". The scene was something from Earth, Wind, and Fire's "Boogie Wonderland":

> *"...the mirror stares you in the face and says*
> *Baby uh, uh, it don't work."* (Earth)

---

[8] This refers to beer in quart bottles.

At 23, I was broke, busted, and disgusted with how I looked. Nevertheless, that was the reality check I needed to get myself back on track.

The next day, I headed to the gym. My start was rather slow because it had been a while since I was serious about exercise. The weights seemed heavier than what I remembered and the track seemed to have been extended. Oh, and the initial pain from the first workout was excruciating. I really wanted to quit and remain a "b", but I didn't. I went back the next day and the next, until it was a habit. On the road back to fitness, I found that there were many people encouraging me to keep moving forward. My gym time increased and the 32 ounce curls decreased. I felt better about myself and about the way I looked. When I walked past my reflection, I would smile, and then give the "click-and-the gun" to the man in the mirror. I was now making sure I took care of myself.

A few months later I received orders for Comiso Air Station, Italy. I had to first complete training at Davis Mothan AFB, AZ. For four months of technical and field training, we spent numerous hours between the classroom, physical training, and the field. The physical training (PT) was the most fun. We would hang out until well past midnight and get up the next morning for PT. At the crack of dawn we were on the field getting ready to be tortured by Sergeant Rock. That wasn't his real name. I don't remember his real name. What I do remember is that he looked like he had a 44 inch waist that was rock solid. He would lie flat on his back and hold his leg six inches from the ground for what seemed like an eternity. We would also be lying on our backs trying to duplicate his actions. Needless to say, as we attempted to mimic Sergeant Rock, everything we had drunk the night before was coming out of every orifice in our bodies. While the PT was physically demanding, it was also invigorating and it built my confidence.

By the end of the four months most of us were in shape. I often joke and say that the only fat on my body was in my ear lobes and lips. Even those who were considered "big boned" seemed to have slimmed down. Slimming down was only a by-product of a healthier lifestyle; it wasn't the goal. In order to pass the training, we had to readjust our thinking and our actions. We realized, in order to get through the 18-hour days of field training, we had to prepare ourselves by being serious about getting in shape. We knew it would not happen by accident. It would take commitment to the program. It was a commitment to taking care of ourselves.

While I was stationed at Hill AFB, UT, a fellow Chief[9] gave me some good advice. He said, "If you don't take care of yourself, you're probably not doing a good job of taking care of others." What he said struck a chord within me. For years I thought that you should take care of others first. However, the logic was so simple and yet so profound. How I can do my best to help others when I'm not at my best? It reminds me of the Michael Jackson song, "Got Me Working Day and Night":

"You Got Me Workin'
Day And Night
And I'll Be Workin'
From Sun Up To Midnight
You Got Me Workin' Workin' Day And Night"
(Jackson)

We have family members that literally worked themselves to death. These wonderful people are the ones that worked two and three

[9] Chief is the Air Force enlisted rank of Chief Master Sergeant (E-9)

jobs trying to support grown folk that should be supporting themselves. After working extended hours, they would spend two to three evenings a week at church praying for those same grown folk. After all the work and prayer, these saints would go home and try to get some rest, but they can't because the grown folks have the house out of order and in disarray (Can you tell that lazy grown folks get on my nerves?). This type of lifestyle may seem noble; however, not caring for ourselves can be harmful and sometimes deadly.

Now, to further stress my point, I like using the example of a flight attendant giving safety instruction prior to departure. The passengers are told in the event oxygen masks drop from the ceiling, make sure to secure their own mask before assisting other passengers or children. The rationale is when you secure your mask first, you will continue to breathe oxygen, be coherent, and be able to better assist others. But you may say, "Put the mask on the children first!" It sounds good, yet if you pass out while trying to help a child, you and the child now need help. Additionally, the people who you could have helped are still in need of help. The bottom line is to take care of yourself so that you can better take care of others.

Taking care of yourself also includes going to sleep. When my cousins and I would spend the night with Ma Gussie, we would spend the day playing outside. When the sun set, Ma Gussie and her neighbor Ms. Daisy would sit on the front porch and reminisce while we continued to play in the yard. Next, we would go inside and take a much needed bath. Then we put on our pajamas, watched a little television, and eventually go to bed. The three of us, without complaining, piled in the bed and continued to play. Hearing our noise, Ma Gussie would say, "Go to sleep!" As kids, we would ignore her first request. Next, she would grab the switch[10] that was next to her bed. I really think she was playing a game with us, because if she wanted, she could have taken that switch and ripped us up. Instead she would pop us a couple of times and we would quiet down and fall asleep.

At that time, I didn't understand the importance of sleep. I thought going to sleep was punishment for something that I had done earlier. As an adult, I've found that sleep is a precious commodity. When used properly, it can reenergize, revitalize, and refresh you.

---

[10] Usually a long flexible limb from a bush or tree.

Many people feel as though they need to go non-stop for as long as they can. They start the day with coffee in the morning, an energy drink at lunch, and natural herb in the evening. At some point the body begins to break down. Reduced sleep was found to be associated with increased risk of diabetes, hypertension, cardiovascular disease and mortality. (The Journal of Environmental and Public Health)

During the funeral services of family members who constantly worked, no one says, "If only they had worked harder." Usually someone would say, "I told them to slow down and take it easy, but they wouldn't listen." Being remembered as a hard worker is a good thing. It helps to instill a good work ethic into future generations. Taken literally, this epitaph gives little consolation to those who are left behind grieving. So the next time a loved one says "I'm tired" or "I'm worn out" tell them what Ma Gussie said, "Go to sleep."

> ...the body begins to breakdown

Before you go too far, let me say that proper sleep is what I'm referring to when I say you should get ENOUGH sleep. Health providers have stated that adults need 6 to 8 hours sleep nightly and children need more. (US Department of Health and Human Services) This is not a hard rule to be followed by everyone. Personally, if I sleep for 8 hours, I wake up feeling tired. My optimal sleep time is 6-7 hours. Find your optimal sleep time and stick with it. The opposite to not getting enough sleep is oversleeping, which can lead to laziness. Similar to over working, laziness can lead to heart disease, diabetes, and hypertension. In Daddy and Momma's house, laziness was not an option. If you wanted to be lazy, you had to work at it. You had to keep moving to find a place where you could hide and try not to do anything. To me, being lazy was counterproductive, so I decided to keep it moving......and you should too. The bottom line is to find a balance and get ENOUGH sleep.

Taking care of yourself does not happen by happenstance. It also does not happen by good intentions. We all have an obligation to take care of each other and that obligation starts with taking care of ourselves.

Did You Hear What I Said?

1. Instead of trying to lose weight, concentrate on being healthy.
2. Don't wear yourself thin, nor wear yourself out.
3. Get some sleep…but not too much.

It Runs in the Family

I n school, there were some classes that were more interesting than others. For me, Biology was one of those classes. We learned about hereditary traits, DNA, phenotypes, and genotypes, and so on. Although the class was interesting, some of the information was memorized, regurgitated on the test, then delete from my memory banks. One part that captured my attention was how certain traits are passed on from generation to generation. Hair color, eye color, baldness, and height are some of the traits that we inherit.

Also, because of our genetic makeup, there are some thing that we are more prone to encounter such as diabetes, hypertension, and heart disease to name a few. This is where the expression, "It runs in the family" comes into play and sometimes stereotypes run rampant.

In the 60's and 70's, Albany was a stereotypical southwest Georgia town. We lived near The Post[11]. As a teen I ventured across the river[12] to Albany State College, the bowling alley, and to visit a few friends. Other than that, I stayed mostly on my side of town. I went to predominately black schools (we weren't African American until later), and our church and neighborhood were totally black. Therefore most of the people that I knew fell into three ethnic categories: Blacks, Whites, and Others. My knowledge of other groups outside of my circle was slim to none. This changed when I enlisted in the Air Force and became more familiar with the why America is called the "melting pot." I became friends with several of

---

[11] American Legion Post 512 was commonly known as "The Post"

[12] Albany was divided by the Flint River. We lived on the south side of town. Those who lived on the east side of town lived "across the river."

my comrades and I learned a great deal about them and their families.

One thing I learned about my friend's families was that diabetes was not germane to Black families. It ran is some of the White, Hispanic, and Asian families also. I realized all families have health issues. The Center for Disease Control reported that between 1990 and 2010, the number of cases of diabetes in the US tripled. The report also stated that 7.1% of Whites, 8.4% of Asians, 11.8% Hispanics and 12.6% of African Americans had been diagnosed with diabetes. (Control) This disease is an issue for America as a nation and not just a certain ethnic groups.

I must add that when I was younger, my understanding of diabetes was very limited. At one time, when I was very young, the disease was known as "The Shougga." I knew that several family members had it, but I didn't take the time to find out what it really meant. I also knew that it "ran in the family". With that in mind, my prayer was, "Lord, don't let me get "The Shougga". As I got older I started gaining a better understanding because I noticed that more and more people I knew were affected by the disease. The numbers of cases of diabetes is continuing to rise each year. This tells us, we are losing ground and losing loved ones to a disease that in some cases is preventable and treatable. Let's work together to break "Shougga's" legs so it doesn't continue to run in the family.

High blood pressure was another disease that "ran in the family". At almost every family get together, someone would eventually say, "I'll be back. I've got to go take my blood pressure medicine." This had become as normal as asking someone to pass the hot sauce. I don't remember questioning anyone about their high blood pressure because it was expected that certain people would always have high blood pressure. In addition to that, some of those same people would inevitably do something to make their pressure go up. They would get into an argument about something; most of the time the argument was about nothing. Next, they would overindulge at mealtime. Their first round would be two slabs of ribs (pork, not beef), a plate of collard greens (seasoned with ham hocks), some butter

> *"I've got to go take my blood pressure medicine."*

soaked corn bread, half of a sweet potato pie, and a tall glass of really sweet tea. As I look back, I realize that one of the reasons "it runs in the family" is not only because of genetics, but also because of lifestyle choices.

When talking about eating habits, I have to talk about Daddy. In many ways I am just like Daddy and that's a good thing. He was a handsome man, lean, and six feet tall. For some reason, the gene for height didn't crossover to me. He also passed on other things such as a great work ethic, a strong sense of responsibility, and a compassionate heart. However, one trait that I could not carry forward was his eating habits. Let me give you an idea of what he would eat on a typical day:

- Morning – Bacon, eggs (cooked in the bacon grease), toast (buttered), and coffee.
- Until noon he would chew Red Man Long Leaf Chewing Tobacco™

- Lunch – Vienna Sausages™, a honey bun, hoop cheese (this was the cheese on the counter at the neighborhood store), and a Coke™ or RC Cola™.
- More chewing tobacco

- Dinner – Fried chicken, black-eyed peas, rice, and sweet tea. When Momma baked a cake, he would eat half of it if she didn't say something.

This menu was not every day, but it wasn't out of the norm. As he got older, he had to change some of his habits. Momma and Diane (my sister) would get on him about his nutrition. To avoid their harassment, he would eat what he wanted before he came home (bless his heart). If I were to try to imitate Daddy's eating habits, I would probably get "The Shougga" and high blood pressure. Amazingly, Daddy didn't have problems with diabetes. His blood pressure was high, however, there were other contributing factors besides his meal choices. I hope that I have his genetic makeup when it comes to not being susceptible to certain diseases. Still, I won't put all my eggs in that basket nor will I fry them in bacon grease like he did.

Because of my size, some people have said, "You're small. You don't have to worry about stuff like diabetes." I have to laugh when I hear that because that's the type of thinking that will make you the honoree at the next memorial service. Imagine if I had Daddy's eating habits AND a predisposition for diabetes and hypertension. I would look okay, but my body would be a walking time bomb on the inside. I have to admit that as an African-American male over 50 years old, and with a family history of certain diseases, I cannot just hope and pray that everything will be alright. I have a responsibility to take charge of my life and work to prevent illnesses versus managing illnesses.

One way to take charge is to make a conscious effort to adhere to portion control. Let's go back to the family get together scenario. An example of portion control would be to eat *two or three* bones of ribs, *one* serving of collards, *a slice* of cornbread, and *a slice* of sweet potato pie. Another way to monitor portion control is to look at the plate itself. Food should not fall from the sides of the plate. If you're walking away from the serving table and the juice from the collards is dripping on your summer suit, you've probably overloaded the plate. Also, even

> **Adhere to portion control**

though it's not written, I do believe that each paper plate has a weight limit. Once you've reached the plate's weight limit, you should not retrieve a second plate to help support the single faltering plate. This is clearly a sign saying you should cease from increasing the height of the food mound. The bottom line is to not stuff yourself until you can't eat another bite.

If you happen to be on the committee for the next family reunion, be that person to say, "Let's try to make the menu healthier." It is not mandatory for each item to be fried, slathered in sauce, or sweeter than sweet. Think about those family members that are struggling with food choices. Instead of collards cooked with ham hocks, try collards with smoked turkey legs and other seasonings. Also suggest that some fresh vegetables and fruit available. This last idea may get you kicked off the committee, but try it anyway. Ask the family to consider water AND less sweetened tea. Remember, the goal is the make the menu healthy-ER.

Obesity is the third thing that runs in the family. This subject is polarizing. Because of my small stature, I am very careful with my choice of words. Sometimes those of us who have not struggled with being overweight, sound judgmental when talking with those who are struggling. Also, there have been times where my good intentions did more harm than good. We have family and loved ones that struggle with being overweight. From home to school to church, obesity has been accepted as the norm. When talking about obesity, I am talking about health, not looks. Media can make you think that anything past size 4 for women or anything past a 30 inch waist for men would be considered overweight. I am referring to overall health.

Obesity has become a problem, not only for adults but among children. Statistics on childhood obesity are staggering. Mission Readiness is a non-profit organization that seeks to reduce childhood obesity and help children become healthier. In a 2012 report, they stated "about 1 in 4 young adults is too overweight to join the military (Mission Readiness). This lets us know that childhood obesity is not just a family issue, but it is a national security issue. Yes, it's that serious. However, we can do something about it.

As I've said earlier, we need to make better choices. In 2008, our family started a 5K Run/Walk to be included in each reunion. We understood that one way to stop things from "running in the family" was to become a family that runs. It was great to see children and seasoned relatives get out and run (actually, most of us walked because it was too hot to be running). At the end we congratulated each other for finishing. The message of the 5K is expressed in III John 1:2:

"… I pray that all may go well with you and that you may be in good health, just as it is well with your soul." (New English Translation)

Did You Hear What I Said?

1. Some things don't have to run in the family.
2. Don't just watch what you eat, control it also.
3. What you eat is a choice, so choose wisely.

Get Up Off That Thang

James Brown was called "the hardest working man in show business." His performances left you wondering how one man could have so much energy. Everything was "on the one."[13] Even the musicians worked hard. Their performances were so intense that you weren't sure if they were sweating from the drugs, from the playing,

---

[13] In James Brown's music, any change happened on the first beat of a four count measure.

or both. Those performers really knew how to put in the work. I tried my best to imitate the Godfather's (as James was called) dance moves. I would glide across the floor, do a split, get up and keep dancing. Unfortunately, I never received any trophies or awards for my efforts, so I kept trying to "get on the good foot."[14] At that time, I didn't think about the health benefits of aerobic exercise. Dancing didn't seem like exercise, it was just fun to get up and move to the music. As James would say:

"Get up offa that thang
Dance and you'll feel better" (Brown)

In addition to dancing, I went outside to play. In 2007, the NFL launched its "Play 60" program which encouraged kids to play for at least 60 minutes a day. (NFL) Are you kidding me? Nowadays, children have to be encouraged, pumped, and primed to go outside and play? For us, not being able to go outside was considered a punishment because outside was a place of adventure, excitement, and fun. The outside world held far greater opportunities to explore and imagine than being stuck inside

---

[14] James Brown recorded "Get On the Good Foot" in 1972.

watching television. Then again, when you only have three or four channels, the black-and-white television got really boring, really quick. In my opinion, children should not be encouraged to go outside. Rather, if they don't want to willingly go outside, they should be thrown out and the door locked behind them. Kids (and adults) should get outside and experience natural reality instead of staying inside and controlling their avatar in virtual reality.

During my teens, I loved going to the skating rink on Sunday nights. This was a favorite gathering place for youth in the Good Life City[15]. The Sunday evening church service would end between 7:00 and 7:30pm. As soon as the benediction ended, we would get ready to head to the rink. Some of us would pile in my parents' Dodge Dart and make our way to the skating rink. The skating rink, to put it mildly, was not the most up-to-date facility in town. It was located by the

Kids and adults should go outside

---

[15] Albany GA was called "The Good Life City."

railroad tracks. The building resembled an old gymnasium where Ralph Naismith would have invented the game of basketball. From the outside you could see the air conditioning units, but on the inside, you didn't notice they were working. There were two temperatures inside: hot and tropic. The humidity was so high, there was always a slight chance of precipitation and you could almost see the sweat dripping off the walls. Yet, we would get there as soon as we could and stay as long as we could because that was the place to be.

Before I go any further, I must let you know that for two years I raced to the skating rink and never put on a pair of skates. Because of foolish pride, I wouldn't allow anyone to watch me bumbling around the rink like a drunken Inspector Gadget. So instead, I would dance which was a dangerous undertaking. Since the dance floor was in the middle of the rink, the goal for those of us sitting in the stands was to move in between the skaters and try to get to the dance floor without being pummeled. Imagine numerous skaters moving around the rink at a slow to medium pace.

Next, the DJ pulled the 12-inch version of Le Freak[16] from the plastic milk carton crate. Once the needle hit the record, the skaters went into overdrive. Needless to say, multiple collisions resulted in several embarrassing moments and a few minor injuries. In spite of danger and embarrassment everyone in the rink skating and dancing.

Sir Isaac Newton concluded that objects in motion tend to stay in motion. This is a key principle for healthy living. As stated earlier, skating and dancing were not associated with exercise because it was fun, and more importantly, it was inexpensive. I laugh sometimes when I think about the amount of money spent on "aerobic activity". A quick search on the internet would garner a plethora of activities that promise to increase your endurance and decrease your body mass index (BMI). Some infomercials make the price

> *Objects in motion tend to stay in motion*

sound reasonable. They use phrases like, "Four easy payments of…" or "…but wait, we'll double

---

[16] Le Freak was recorded by Chic in 1978.

your order!" I have fallen prey to purchasing equipment that became a room fixture or an alternative place to hang clothes. I came to the realization that for zero money down and zero monthly payments, I could have gone outside and worked in the yard for free. If you look around the house there are many things you can do to increase your heart rate:

- Wash and detail the car
- Mow the grass
- Plant and maintain a garden
- Clean the garage

Doing these types of activities will make you feel better, make your house look better and you will also save you a little money in the process.

Daddy was a man who stayed in motion most of the time. His philosophy was to get up and get moving. Before the crack of dawn he would be up, dressed, and ready to go work. My morning was a little different. I would lie in bed until the last possible minute. Then I would hear the noise from the percolator and smell the coffee brewing. That's when I knew that it was only a matter of time before Daddy would knock once on the bedroom door and say, "WAYNE...let's go." Just like the Army slogan, "we would do more before 9 am than most people did all day." After a long day of work, we arrived home tired and ready to relax. Without our knowledge, we had completed both our aerobic an anaerobic workouts. Understanding the importance of this principle is something that would elude me for years. Once I got the concept, I was able to improve my health and get more things accomplished.

When it came to keeping it moving, Daddy wasn't my only influence. I was also surrounded by others that felt the need to get up before the rising sun. Uncle Sam, Daddy's younger brother, was one of those people. He worked at a local dry cleaners and he had a side hustle.[17] At the dry cleaners, he was always on the move cleaning clothes, working the front counter, and delivering clothes to VIPs. His work ethic enabled him to move from employee to being the owner of the dry cleaners. Between Daddy and Uncle Sam, I had no choice but to keep it moving. In addition to that dynamic duo, there were carpenters, electricians, factory workers, and hustlers who were examples of people in motion. Yes, even the hustlers knew that lying in bed was not

---

[17] A "side hustle" was another job in addition to the main job.

good for business. Movement was paramount to being successful, no matter the occupation.

While many people around me were constantly on the move, many of them still developed health problems. One factor for the ailments was that some did not make regular visits to the doctor. For those in my parents' generation, going to the doctor was not always an option. Lack of health insurance and being unable to find a trustworthy physician hindered them from getting regular checkups. In 1932, the Tuskegee Experiment was a study that was conducted to examine the effects of syphilis in African-American males. The men were not informed of the purpose of the study nor were they properly treated for the disease. The study lasted until 1972. (Washington) As you could imagine, many African American males did not want to see any physician. However, this reasoning does not negate the fact that regular checkups are a life saver.

Early detection of some illnesses can prevent them from being fatal. Below is a list of checkups that everyone should have (CDC):

- Breast and Cervical Cancer Early Detection
- Cholesterol
- Colorectal Cancer Screening

- Diabetes
- High Blood Pressure
- Immunizations
- Oral Health
- Prostate Cancer Screening
- Skin Cancer Screening
- HIV/AIDS

This is not an all-inclusive list; however, if you start with the exams on the list, you will be well on your way to a healthier life.

When looking at the list, I am sure that some of the exams may make you cringe. For the ladies, PAP smears are not the most comfortable exams. Being invaded by Draconian looking tools can make some women have panic attacks prior to the exam. For the fellas, the two most intrusive exams are the prostate exam and the colonoscopy. If you thought the prostate exam was scary, then make sure to ask the anesthesiologist to put you under prior to going into the exam room for the colonoscopy. On the day of my exam, they wheeled me into the hallway of the exam room. Next, one doctor came out to let me know about the procedure and to answer any questions. Then they took me into the examination room and the anesthesiologist talked to me about the medication I'd receive (he should have given me the drugs at that point). Afterwards, a technician showed me the apparatus they would be using to perform the exam. I cannot fully describe how I felt, but I will say that I started whining like Lassie[18] the dog. That's when they gave me the drugs and told me to count backwards from 20. When I woke up, the exam was over and I had no recollection of what happened. Although that wasn't something I looked forward to, it was something that was needed.

When we want to, we can always find an excuse for not doing what we know is best. Getting up, getting out, and getting to the doctor are things we must do if we want to be around to see future generations. Personally, I don't just want to be around to "see" future generations, I want to be able to interact with them and enjoy their company. I also want to live to see a time when at family reunions, there are several tables reserved for the elders who are 90 years and older. In case you're wondering, yes I plan to be there.

---

[18] "Lassie" was a television show about a female dog.

Did You Hear What I Said?

1. Get up and move.
2. Get to the doctor for regular checkups.
3. Get rid of the excuses.

EMOTIONAL

WAYNE S. BROWN

Laugh, Forgive, and Live

Some things in life are hilarious. Here's a little ditty that I thought would make you laugh:

There once was a teen named Tom,
Who felt like he'd just ate a bomb.
He passed some gas,
His pants gained a stain,
He felt like he'd sat in some napalm.[19]

---

[19] Napalm was a gel mixture used in bombs and flame throwers in the Vietnam Conflict.

The teen's real name is Wayne and the events in the poem really happened. I was on a church trip when one of the most embarrassing moments in my life took place. Early that morning, I woke up that morning and went to breakfast. I don't remember what we ate, but I do know that it was not well with my soul. Just before we started boarding the bus I felt my stomach beginning to bubble. I didn't want to use the restroom because it was dirty and I didn't want anyone to hear me making sounds like a WWII bombing raid. In other words, I didn't want to be embarrassed.

As the poem stated, that didn't work out for me. I tried to convince everyone that I sat in something. Actually, I was telling the truth because I did sit in something. Then I had to go to the bus driver and ask him to unlock the bus so I could change clothes. He and the other adults tried not to laugh too hard. Finally I got changed and went on with my day. When I looked back on that day, I have to admit that it was gut-bustin' funny.

Another one of my embarrassing moments came when I raised my voice at Daddy. The fact that I am able to write this book is proof positive that God is merciful to the simple. The scene starts with me driving home from church with Daddy sitting in the passenger seat. A car was approaching us in the other lane. Daddy told me to move over to avoid an oncoming car. Evidently I didn't move over far enough for him. Upon giving the instructions the second time, he raised his voice and told to me move over. Instead of moving over, I decided to tell him that I'd already moved over.

Next, we exchanged a few words and when we arrived at home I got out of the car first and slammed the door behind me (not a smart move). In the house, I felt like Braveheart[20] and I prepared for battle. When Daddy came into the house he looked like a man on a mission. Then he said the words I will never forget. He calmly told me, "You and I are going back outside. I'll forget that I'm your Daddy and that you're my son. We'll just be two men outside fighting". I didn't know what to do. I could feel the testosterone ebbing from my body and my masculinity rapidly decreasing. Momma just stood there and wouldn't step in to save me. The Gospel had not been preached in the whole world, therefore the rapture seemed like it wasn't going to happen anytime soon. So I

---

[20] Braveheart was a movie about William Wallace who led the Scots in battle against England.

stood there praying that Daddy would remember that I was not only his son, but also remember that I was the baby. After a few minutes his anger subsided and God's mercy prevailed.

While these events were happening (and shortly thereafter), I did not see anything comical. Now when I tell the stories, I get a kick out of watching people laugh so much that they start crying. Laughter is an indicator that you've moved past some not-so-funny moments in your life. Have you ever been in a group where someone tells a story and everyone laughs except the main character in the story? Their lack of laughter may be an indicator that they haven't fully gotten past that event. For them, the sting of embarrassment or hurt hasn't been removed. Therefore, they cannot join in the fun or initiate any joking when it comes to that event. Comedians are masters at turning their pain into laughter. Their purpose is to give laughter to others even at their own expense. This type of defense mechanism has

> *Laughter is an indicator that you've moved on*

helped me cope with painful moments in my life; and I've had many. Being able to laugh at yourself and making others laugh, while sharing a valuable lesson makes the pain subside and reaffirms Proverbs 17:22,

"A joyful heart is good medicine, but a broken spirit dries up the bones." (New American Standard Bible)

Being able to laugh at a painful situation can also mean that you've learned how to forgive. After some time had passed, Daddy and I could laugh about that time I decided to "get froggy." One reason is because he forgave me for that moment of stupidity. If he would have held that against me, he would have continued to relive the anger of that moment and be bound in time, never to move forward. Many people walk around holding on to anger from something done in their past. Holding on to resentment can lead to some illnesses. Studies have been conducted on women with breast cancer. The results showed that women's emotions had a direct effect on their treatment and recovery (Giese-Davis). I, for one, have chosen to let go of the anger and resentment that resulted from past hurts. Now I am able to enjoy life without recalling the hurt every time someone mentions certain events.

In 2006 our oldest daughter, Ouidaintria, graduated from college with her Master degree went to the graduation. On the day of celebration, guests filled the tiny apartment. The guest list included: Laura and I, along with our youngest daughter Tasha, our granddaughter Serenity, Grandfather Irenus (Daddy), Auntie Diane, Pam (her mom), and Reed (Tasha's dad). If this were a reality show, it would have been an episode full of drama. The show would start off with Laura shouting at Reed because he didn't do right by Tasha. On the other side of the room, Pam and I would be arguing about something that happened when Ouidaintria was in elementary school. Then Granddaddy and Auntie Diane would join the milieu because they needed to get something off of their chest. Instead of the graduation being a joyous and wonderful occasion, we would have turned it into a No Holds Barred, Iron Cage match.

Forgiveness always triumphs over hurt and pain. Instead of the reality show scene, we all spent the time laughing and celebrating. In fact, the laughter throughout the apartment was so genuine, an outsider would not have been aware of the dynamics of the relationships. You have to learn to forgive others and you must learn to forgive yourself.

> *I had family and friends to help me*

If you've been on the planet for an extended period of time, you probably can make a list of some not-so-stellar moments. The list could range from cheating on an exam to cheating on a loved one. It is interesting to note that the common thread between each item listed will be YOU. Sometimes, to move past these events we have to forgive ourselves. After the demise of my first marriage, I beat myself up over some things that I know I did wrong. I would systematically go through each fault and try to figure out what I could have done to avoid failure. No matter how much I tried, I wouldn't find an answer that would suffice. Since I couldn't find an answer, I beat myself up by doing penance. The problem was that when I finished my penance, I would be emotionally bludgeoned and drained. Fortunately for me, I had family members and friends that helped me through those times. The process wasn't completed overnight. Over time I learned that I can't go back, but, I can go forward and not repeat the same blunders. I recognized that I had to move forward and not waste time trying to fix the past.

Time is a precious commodity. The past is long gone, the present is fleeting, and the future is sometimes uncertain. Therefore, we cannot waste time being a Monday Morning Quarterback. After Sunday's big game, every quarterback can wake up Monday and say, "I should've thrown that pass earlier...", "I could've read the defense better..." or "I should've called timeout when..." He can't transport himself back in time and neither can we. Each and every moment leads us to our present situation and sets us up for future situations. Darius Rucker sums it up in the chorus from his song "This":

"All the doors that I had to close
All the things I knew but I didn't know
Thank God for all I missed
'Cause it led me here to this." (Rucker)

We all must do what we can with the time we have. The events of October 5, 2012 etched this principle in my mind. That morning I woke up to get my day started. Our granddaughter

Serenity was getting ready for school. Our daughter LaTasha was getting the youngest granddaughter, Harmony, and our grandson Justice ready to go with her. After LaTasha got Justice ready, she bought him in the room with me and Laura. Justice and I were wrestling with each other until LaTasha was ready to leave. As they were leaving Laura said, "Bye Stinker" and I said, "See you later Sonny." He smiled and laughed. A couple of hours later LaTasha called. She was frantic and I couldn't understand what she was trying to say. When I finally understood what she was saying, I nearly dropped to the floor. She said that Justice wasn't breathing and that she was headed to the hospital. Laura and I jumped in the car and made the 1 ½ hour ride to the hospital.

One the way to the hospital, LaTasha called again to tell us that Justice had died. He was only five months old. When he was born, none of us had a clue that we had only 163 days to enjoy life with Justice. Aaron, his dad, was there when he stopped breathing. He tried to revive him and he had to watch the paramedics try to revive him also. For LaTasha, by the time she arrived at the hospital, it was too late. For Laura and I, we had to drive at a snail's pace through the bumper-to-bumper traffic, wishing we could immediately transport ourselves to the hospital. We all had our woulda', coulda', shoulda' moments, but we had to come to the realization that he was gone and we were still here.

During this time, Serenity and Harmony were very inspirational. At ages 6 and 2, they showed everyone that life goes on. One week after the funeral, Serenity was back in school and Harmony was getting up and wanting to play. They both had lost their only brother, yet they had the fortitude to move forward. Don't get stuck in time trying to recreate moments that will never come back. Cherish the moments you have and look forward to moments to come.

Did You Hear What I Said?

1. Don't get mad when others laugh at your embarrassing moments. Understand they are laughing ......BECAUSE IT'S FUNNY!!!
2. Forgive others and yourself. It makes life more enjoyable.
3. Redeem the time because it's one thing that you can't get back.

Be Responsible for Your Actions

The internet has connected people on every continent. We can hear and read stories about the lives of people in cultures that are much different from our own. Yet, we can and find commonalities between each other. I believe that one of those cross-cultural commonalities is being responsible for your actions. No matter what part of the world you are in, everyone is responsible for themselves. This is a part of being an adult and sometimes it coincides in certain cultures with rites of passage. For young girls, the Debutante Ball, the Quinceanera, and the Bat Mitzvah are celebrations that mark the girl's transition from child to young adult.

Unfortunately, the Bar Mitzvah is one of only a few traditions that were passed down, which celebrate this transition for young boys. A major part of these celebrations is that the honoree is now more responsible for what they say and do.

Taking responsibility for your actions is not something that happens automatically. Do you remember being caught doing something you were told not to do? I can't count how many times my response was, "Everybody else was doing it." One stern response would come in the form of a question, "If everybody jumped off the bridge, would you jump too?" I really wanted to answer, "YES", but because most people knew I couldn't swim, I kept my mouth shut.

Since the beginning of time, people have been pushing their responsibilities towards something or someone else. Genesis 3 is evidence of this fact. Adam and Eve were in the Garden of Eden. Everything was perfect. The environment was free from global warming and pollution. The waters were pure and flowed throughout the garden. They even talked with

God in the cool of the day. God gave them a commandment to not eat from the tree of the knowledge of good and evil. Instead of obeying God's command, they decided to eat the fruit of the tree. When approached by God, Adam said that it was Eve's fault. When God spoke to Eve, she blamed it on the serpent. Neither person took responsibility for their failure to obey. Over two thousand years later, we are still dealing with the consequences of their actions.

In the early 70's, the comedian Flip Wilson had a variety show. One of his on-stage personas was the "round-the-way-girl," Geraldine. She was a full of life character that said exactly what was on her mind. When pressured to answer for her actions she would say, "The devil made me do it." (Biography) For Flip, this was comedy imitating life. Unfortunately, for too many people, this has become life imitating buffoonery. We are bombarded daily with talk shows, editorials, and books on how someone else is the blame for everything that is wrong with the world. If I'm overweight, it's because McDonald's

> **Neither person took responsibility**

commercials made me eat all those burgers. If I can't read, it's because the library closes too early for me to checkout any books. If I'm emotionally maladjusted, it's because my parents didn't buy me a car when I was a teenager.

As a volunteer in the schools and community, I see this same scenario played out over and over again. If the child or the school is failing, some of the parents say t's the teachers' fault because they are the people responsible for teaching the children and making sure they pass the test. Some teachers say it's the parents' fault because they don't take time to help their children at home. People in the community say it's the government's fault because it doesn't support the schools with enough funding. Lastly, the government officials say it's the economy's fault because they are forced to make budget cuts. During all of the blame shifting, the children and the school continue their downward spiral and little is accomplished. This cyclical projection only ends when we all take responsibility for ourselves.

In the summer of 2013, a Texas teenager went to a party with some friends. At the party, they were drinking and ended up intoxicated.

One bad decision led to another and the teens got in a truck and left the party. At the same time, there was a mother and daughter who were stopped on the side of the road. A responsible man stopped to help them. Within minutes, the drunken teens' vehicle crashed into the immobile car. The ending result was four people dead and nine people injured. The driver and owner of the vehicle took a plea bargain and plead guilty to manslaughter. The judge sentenced the teen to 10 years' probation and therapy at an in-patient facility. The maximum allowable sentence was 20 years in prison. However, his attorney claimed that the teen should not be held responsible for his actions due to "affluenza". Here's the dictionary definition:

Also called: sudden-wealth syndrome. The guilt or lack of motivation experienced by people who have had or inherited large amounts of money.
(Merriam-Webster)

Because of his family's wealth and his parent's unwillingness to set boundaries, the teen was not totally at fault. He was a product of his environment. Here's a news flash, "This just in...we have breaking news that doctors have found the cause of thousands of low income young men and women being incarcerated. The disease is called "Brokial asthma". Here's the definition:

The propensity for being lethargic due to the lack of tangible capital. In extreme cases a person may experience labored breathing due to stress and anxiety(mymeaning.com)

To go along with brokial asthma, here's imaginary an incident that may explain irrational behavior. A parishioner was found "not guilty" for fatally shooting her pastor. Her defense team argued that the she suffered from an acute case of "offendicitis".

The inclination for sudden outbursts of anger experienced, by teens and adults, who are challenged by any type of authority.

Things are so far out of hand that I don't have to take responsibility for making up these terms. These phony medical diseases are the product of a large cup of coffee and my mother's cynical wit. It's not my fault. At some point we have to say enough is enough.

When children are being potty trained, they try their best to take control of their bodily functions. They are at a transition point where they don't want to be seen as being a baby. At this time, the bulge from the diaper inside their pants is neither cute nor comfortable. This is also a time where the child wants more independence. The process can be very messy. The child may or may not make it to the pot in time. When they don't make it to the potty, they leave a trail of urine and fecal deposits to be cleaned. Finally, the day comes when they can go on their own. They are so proud of their success that they want everyone to see what they've done. Everyone stands around and claps for the replica of a volcanic island that sits in the middle of the pot. Now the child has moved up from diapers to their "big kids" underwear.

As adults, we need to put on our "big boys" and "big girls" undies when it comes to taking responsibility for our actions. I understand that there are situations where people have little or no choice. I am not referring to these people or situations. I'm talking about the times where you receive good information, you have time to ask questions and get clarification, and you make a decision to act. In these cases, you are responsible for the actions and/or the inactions.

It is asinine to blame others for our irresponsibility. Here is a personal example. I have been in situations where someone was being verbally abused and I did not say or do anything. I stood there and watched that person being emotionally dismantled. All it would have taken to change the situation was for me to say, "That's enough." Instead, I rationalized my inaction and let it continue. I used the saying "stay out of other folks business" as my excuse for my failure to act. Truthfully, it was my lack of courage that immobilized me. Fortunately, there was no fighting and the person who was abused moved on past the incident. However, the outcomes did not negate the fact that I should have done something.

> *It is asinine to blame others for our irresponsibility.*

You may be thinking, "I would have said something." Maybe you would have, and maybe not. How many times a day have we passed by situations where we know a person needed assistance. They may need a ride, some food, or someone to intervene. Then, instead of providing assistance, we keep it moving because we feel that we don't have time to stop. In Luke 10:25-37, Jesus tells a parable of three people on a treacherous road from Jerusalem to Jericho. A man traveling the road was attacked by robbers. The first person, a Priest, saw the man on the side of the road and kept it moving. The second person, a Levite, did the same thing. The third man, a Samaritan, stopped to help the man. All three had a responsibility to do something, but only one person did something to help. The English orator and politician Edmund Burke is credited for saying,

"All that is necessary for the triumph of evil is that good men do nothing."

I've been that guy that did nothing. It's a horrible feeling to know that you had the power to change a situation for the better and you did nothing. That type of guilt weighs on the heart.

Responsibility can be a heavy load. The load does get easier to bear when we accept the fact that it's your load. If you want to lighten that load, then start by examining your actions and their consequences. By doing this you can see where mistakes were made. Once the mistakes are identified, you can develop solutions to fix what was broken and ensure that you don't repeat the same bad decisions. Taking these steps is far more productive than going on social media and telling the world the reason you've made so many bad decisions is because of the people around you. Let's grow up and start moving forward.

Did You Hear What I Said?

1. Unless you're under duress, you are totally responsible for what you do.
2. At some point you should put on your big kids undies.
3. If you see something wrong, don't just walk by….fix it.

Relationships

O n Saturday afternoon, Don Cornelius would invade households across the country with the hippest trip in America. You had to make sure and watch Soul Train because you didn't want to go to school on Monday morning and not know who performed. You did what you had to do in order to watch the show. If you had chores, it meant you actually cleaned up and did everything you were told. If it was homework, you made sure it was done. When I was 11, one of the shows featured The Main Ingredient.

Their hit was, "Everybody Plays the Fool". Check out some of the lyrics:

"(spoken) Okay, so your heart's been broken
You sit around mopin'
Cryin' and cryin'
You say you even think' about dyin'
Well, before you do anything rash, dig this
(chorus)
Everybody plays the fool, sometimes
No exceptions to the rules" (Ingredient)

As a young boy, I didn't realize that this song would become increasingly true as I got older. High school was a very awkward time. At 16, I was five foot nothing, weighed a hundred and nothing, and my voice was so high that singing soprano was easy. I remember driving to school and parking close to the back so no one could see that I was sitting on books. This was before tilt steering wheels and it was the only way I could see over the dash. Needless to say, my self-confidence wasn't booming through the roof. There were girls that I liked, but I couldn't get that dating thing together. I was also slow when it came to getting the hint. Unless a girl specifically said she liked me, I missed the subtle hints and word play. I'm pretty sure that some of the girls decided that I was too much work.

Along with being awkward, money was another issue for me. I had a job and always had a little money in my pockets, and it seemed that dating would considerably reduce my finances. Lastly, I saw my friends go through hell and back with the constant nagging, arguing, and emotional rollercoaster. Now that I'm in my 50's, I don't think I missed out on much.

When I go into the schools or talk with youth groups, I try to find out the current rules for dating. Each time I ask about the rules, I get a different answer. Some say that the rules depend on who you're with. That means that everything is relative. You may have an exclusive or inclusive relationship. Exclusive would mean that you will be given a list of people (male and female) that you cannot associate with. If the relationship is inclusive, you will still have the same type of list; only shorter. That is very confusing to me. I was hoping that the dating game had gotten less complex. Instead it appears to have gotten more complicated. During my teens, there was no social media, no cell phones, and no unlimited anytime minutes on the one and only phone in the house. If you wanted to keep up with someone, then it took a lot of effort. You had to have lookouts that would give you the rundown of your boo's whereabouts. I didn't have the desire or the time to keep up with anyone. That coupled with the fact that I wasn't the sharpest pencil when it came to the opposite sex, meant that I didn't get many phone calls. Usually, I ended up being a girl's "friend" or "buddy". This meant that she really wanted to hook up with one of my cousins or one of my friends. This type of rejection was not something that I welcomed. No young man wants to be "friends" with a girl he's attracted to and he definitely doesn't want to see her with someone else. Oh the days of unrequited love.

When I talk with young people today, it seems that they don't take this type of rejection very well. It's almost as if a certain person is not interested in a having an exclusive relationship, the teen then goes into depression and needs therapy. This mindset then follows the teen into adulthood. I talk to many young (and old) adults that are devastated when they experience unrequited love. Here's some advice; learn to like yourself. If you don't like yourself, you're probably not going to do a good job of liking others. Stop and take inventory on who you are. What do you like about you? Next, make a list of what you don't like about you. Which list is longer? I've heard people say, "You shouldn't think more highly of yourself than you ought!" Talk about taking a scripture out of context. As Daddy would say, "That makes as much sense as two left shoes." If you don't think much of yourself, why shouldn't others follow your lead? In Genesis 2, God states that you are made in His image and His likeness. That makes you very special and you don't have to downplay that fact.

Now that you know that you're special, let's talk about boundaries (sounds better than rules). First rule: You can't just date anybody. Take it from those who have gone on before you, you must be selective. Even the animal kingdom is selective. Those who have less than desirable traits are not allowed to breed and are killed off or left to die. Wildebeests are a good example. Sir David Attenborough narrated a documentary on the great wildebeest migration. Some males roam in bachelor herds. (BBC) If a male is slow and weak, he probably won't be on any of the female's dance card. Why? Only the most suitable males get a chance to mate and pass on their traits. So before you get involved with someone, make sure that you don't waste time on someone who has questionable traits.

When Laura and I met, she ran a check on me. She worked as a Dental Technician. Because of the nature of her job, she had access to personal and pertinent health information, such as communicable diseases (sexually transmitted diseases). As you probably already guessed, the day after we met, Laura checked my records to make sure that I was being truthful and that I wasn't carrying something that a shot couldn't fix. When she told me what she had done, I wasn't the least bit upset. She was a single mom with a daughter she had to think about. There was no sense in being in a relationship that was doomed before it started. Make sure that you check out anyone BEFORE you get into a relationship.

Laura ran a check on me.

The internet gives everyone access to public information. You can search criminal records, tax records, addresses, dependents, marital status and many other key items that you should know beforehand. Don't play the fool. Get that background check. If they get upset, they'll get over it. If, and only if, the person passes the background check, then you can THINK about moving forward. Please don't rush and get into the pseudo-marriage type of relationship. The group Heatwave posed this question in the song "Mind Blowin Decisions":

"Marriage or shacking, which way do we go
One of us must let the other know
By taking our time we will work our problems
out
'Til death do we part or as friends we'll begin...
Mind blowing, decisions,
Causes head on, collisions" (Heatwave)

For you youngsters, "Shackin" was a term we used for people who were not married, but living together. What I find interesting about the concept is that some people say "it's just like being married." If it's just like being married, then get married. Why would you want to pretend when you can "be"?

I must admit that some of us who are married have not been very good examples of having a great marriage. Some people have been married for more than half a century and when you ask them about marriage, they say things such as:

"Marriage is tough, but it's worth it"
"Every marriage has its ups and downs. You take the good with the bad"
"We said for better or worse, so we're gonna tough it out"

I can see why marriage is viewed as a duty and not a delight. I can say that my marriage is not tough. I'm actually married to my best friend. We love each other, laugh with each other, and more importantly, we like each other. God is at the center of our marriage. He has allowed us to grow together in Him and in each other. I'm not talking about some existential experience. I'm simply talking about waking up each morning and being glad that I get to share everyday with my wife. Marriage can be wonderful if you want it to be. Take the time to get to know the person you want to marry. They don't have to be perfect, but, they should be perfect for you.

Relationships are paramount to living the good life. For those who choose to be single, make sure that you choose wisely also. Many of us have jacked up relationships because we didn't understand the power of attraction. Just because you are attracted to someone doesn't mean that your relationship should be romantic. The attraction may come from shared ideas and common goals. This person may be the one to help you fulfill your destiny. As a young man, I had several ladies that were friends and comrades-in-arms. These women helped me in my career, my personal growth, and my spiritual growth. Some of them were easy on the eyes and some not so much. Had I tried to go the romantic route it would have been like dating my sister or a close cousin. Now our connections are still close and I have greatly benefited from our relationships.

Being single also does not mean that you won't go through the same type of drama as married couples. Your relationships can also take you to hell and back. Actually, the same rules apply to platonic relationships also. If someone wants to be a part of your life, they should be vetted. Once they make the cut, then they can have more access. Also, make sure to periodically evaluate your relationships. You should be able to say that since this person has been in your life, your life has gotten better. If they haven't improved some part of your life, then it's probably time to limit or deny them access.

This is especially true with mentor/mentee relationships. Usually the mentee chooses the mentor. When you have that opportunity, make sure you take it seriously. You should choose someone who has been where you want to go. If it's a financial mentor, you should check their financial records. Many people can tell you how to make a million dollars, yet, they can't scrape up $100. If it's a spiritual mentor, verify that their faith is a lifestyle, not just in-style. Aligning yourself with someone who is misaligned can lead to disaster. My checking account can bear witness to the fact that not pursuing due diligence can be a very expensive lesson. With this in mind, listen and learn from my mistakes or don't listen and learn from your own. If you learn from my mistakes, I promise that the lessons will be at least half-price.

Did You Hear What I Said?

1. Don't be in a rush to get involved in a relationship.
2. Learn to "like" yourself.
3. Check people out. If you don't, there's a good chance you'll end up being played.

FINANCIAL

WAYNE S. BROWN

Don't Nobody Owe You Nothing

One thing I like about music is that it allows lyrics to be interpreted by musicians and singers. Popular country singers, Melba Montgomery and Tammy Wynette along with the first lady of Gospel Shirley Caesar, recorded a song entitled "No Charge". Even if you're not a fan of country or gospel, you are moved by their stirring performances. This song is very heartfelt and most people can relate to it. The story is about a child giving their mother an itemized list of the chores that they completed. Included in the list are tasks such as cleaning the room, taking out the trash, and mowing the yard. At the end of the list was a total price of $14.75. The mother wiped her apron and began to calmly give the child a list of things that she had done. Her list included: 9 months of pregnancy, staying up all night during sickness, toys, food, and clothes. At the end of her list the cost was "no charge". (Caesar) The lyrics are simple enough that most people can see that the child didn't understand the mother's daily sacrifice. The child only saw their efforts and the money they expected to receive. While this song was first recorded in 1974, the child's attitude is still prevalent today.

Affirmative Action was implemented to give women and minorities a better chance to compete for advancement opportunities. The laws benefited those groups that have been hindered by discrimination. African-Americans are not the only group to suffer injustice in America. Native Americans were forced from their land and made to march the Trail of Tears. The Suffrage Movement fought for women's voting rights and currently women are fighting just to get equal pay. Asian Americans were confined to Internment Camps during World War II because some in Congress felt that they would not remain loyal to the US.

We live in an imperfect country with imperfect people. Our history is rife with examples of injustice. With this in mind, let's curb the "I suffered more than you" attitude. When I was on active duty, we called it "And One" because it is similar to someone getting fouled in basketball and being rewarded with the basket and the foul shot. You have a headache and the other person has a migraine. You may have a cold and they have walking pneumonia. Enough already.

When Native Americans were forced to leave their homes, they were placed on reservations. If you've never been to a reservation, take a ride through a reservation in Arizona. Although the tribes were given land, you will see that the land wasn't much of a gift. In 1964, President Johnson signed the Civil Rights Act. African American's didn't receive monetary compensation, but it was a step in the right direction. In the late 60's, Affirmative Action allowed women and minorities to attend schools they were previously not allowed to attend. One of the benefactors of Affirmative Action was Dr. Henry Louis Gates. In 1969, he and 96 minority students attended Yale University. He has done extensive work on African American history and has been criticized for his views on slavery. His documentary, "Many Rivers to Cross" discusses how Africans worked with slave traders to enslave fellow Africans. This did not sit well with those who want to selectively blame Europeans only.

Cornelia Brown didn't wait for 40 acres and a mule.

Gates does acknowledge the horrific and long-lasting effects of over 300 years of oppression. There are some people that feel the African American community should be compensated for the crimes of slavery. They are looking for their 40 acres. In his PBS article, "The Truth about 40 Acres and a Mule" Gates explains what happened to the land that was promised to the slaves. The land was given to the slaves by Special Field Order 15. However, less than one year later, the Order was overturned by President Andrew Jackson and the land was returned to its former owners. (PBS) So what about now? Where's my land?

Prior to all of us getting on the bus and going to Washington to demand our land, let's look at what others have done. My great grandmother Cornelia Brown did not sit and wait for someone to give her 40 acres and a mule. In the early 1900's she found herself widowed with four children. Also, she had no right to vote, she was treated as a second class citizen, and we are told that she couldn't read (or maybe she could and felt it best to not let everybody know). With these daunting circumstances, she could have easily sat and did nothing or tried to find a man to take in her and the four children. Instead she used determination and business acumen to make it happen. She talked to the right people and was able to secure money to farm the land. Cornelia and her children could continue to stay on the land and become profitable farmers. My great grandmother received assistance. However, this assistance was given to someone determined to succeed.

Receiving government assistance is a right given to all citizens. However, this entitlement has been often abused. Here's something to ponder, some people feel that if they have a baby, the government is obligated to take care of that child. When did the financial obligation shift from the parents to the government? The key word here is "assistance". If the government is your sole source of income, then you've moved from being "assisted" to being "dependent". When you are a dependent you are always looking to the sponsor for everything. Here's an example of being dependent on the government. Each month a person receives:

- SNAP (Food Stamps for the Ol' School)
- Medicare pays for the medical and dental
- Free or reduced breakfast and lunch.
- Free or reduced childcare
- Free afterschool programs
- Unemployment benefits (for those who didn't get fired)
- Housing

These are just some of the government assistance programs. The private sector has many other programs available for those seeking help.

Along with government and private assistance, some of these same people get assistance from family members. "Momma and them" have been helping out while they are trying to "get themselves together." Life has taught me that family owes you their support, not necessarily their money. I've been involved in several multi-level marketing ventures. Each one tells you to make a list of people that you can contact. Family members are usually the first people on the list. Please note that family members are not obligated to give financial support to every idea that you have. If you're that family member that is contacted, here's what you can do. Ask the petitioner how much money they are willing to invest. If they stutter while trying to answer the question, know that you will end up contributing much more than your one-time donation.

It's time to go from "they owe me" to "what can I do for myself". I've talked with a single mom that told me she hated going to the child services office to get assistance. She also said that within six months she was on her feet and stopped receiving assistance. This is the mentality that you must have in order to be financially stable. Unfortunately, becoming dependent on others sometimes leads to financial laziness. Since you know you will have all the basic needs met, you lose the drive to achieve more. I'm not talking about low income people only. There are many people who grew

> **Family is not obligated to give money to every idea.**

up in homes where they never experienced lack, and for some reason, they have developed a sense of entitlement. Some of them actually think that they have the same financial status as their parents. Here's a news flash, if you're an adult and you can't provide for yourself, you're probably in the low income bracket. Nope, your parent's address does not make you any richer.

Try sitting down and make a list of everyone you owe. The list may include student loans, medical bills, credit cards, unpaid personal loans, etc. Start by paying back the money you owe. One immediate benefit is that your credit score will go up. Another benefit is that you don't have to avoid those annoying phone calls and letters from collection agencies. Also, you will now be able to attend different gatherings (family, church, and school reunions) without having to avoid those you owe. Believe me, it's a good feeling when you don't owe people. Anytime you owe someone or they owe you, the relationship gets complicated. Have you ever seen someone that owes you money, at the mall spending money they say they didn't have? It makes you extremely angry. Now take that feeling and know that when you don't pay your debts, others feel that way about you. The bottom line is that you want to move to being independent.

Proverbs 22:7 states:

"The rich rule over the poor, and the borrower is servant to the lender." (New King James Version)

Being indebted to someone is similar to being their servant. I don't know about you, but I don't wear servitude well. (Side note for you religious people; I am a servant of Jesus Christ, so fix your face). The good thing is that we don't have to be servants. We can get the assistance we need and move on. However, if we take advantage of people and not take advantage of opportunities, we end up being that person that young people talk about when they say, "I don't ever want to end up like them."

Did You Hear What I Said?

1. You probably won't get the 40 acres and a mule.
2. Government assistance is supposed to be temporary.
3. Pay what you owe.

WAYNE S. BROWN

It's Within You

Biology was not my favorite subject, but I have always found it very interesting. Cell division and maintenance caught my attention. When I took Biology in college I got a chance to gain a deeper understanding of cell reproduction. It was fascinating how a single cell can develop into a billion duplicates of itself. Even more exciting was how gametes coming together to form a new cell, then a zygote, then an embryo, and finally a baby. All of these processes automatically take place without asking for permission or assistance. The DNA is pre-coded with all the information needed for the current cell and all proceeding cells. In light of these facts, would it be safe to assume that as multicellular organisms, we also are supplied with everything we need to reproduce and to be successful? As humans we breathe, consume, and produce automatically. We are able to accomplish these things because of the organs that are within us.

Let's go a little further and apply this same logic to another area of our lives; our finances. Early in life, we are told that when we get older, we should find a "good" job so that we can take care of ourselves and our families. A lot of time is spent trying to land that "good" job. I first started working with Daddy cutting grass and doing custodial work at River Road. For a young teen, that was a good job. When I was 16, I started working at Red Lobster™. This job had better pay with more opportunities to work. For a high school student, it was a good job, except for having to take two showers to get rid of the seafood stench.

After high school I landed a "great" job when I enlisted in the Air Force. Benefits, travel, and education; what more could anyone ask. For 30 years, this was my career. If I wanted to try something new, I looked at the list of available jobs and chose the one I thought was exciting or would advance my career. As the twilight of my career approached, I attended seminars and classes that helped me to build my resume and prepare me for job interviews. I found that at 48, I was still trying to get a "good job" with benefits.

Please know that I am all about hard, honest work. I am not against having a good job. There are many people who provide all of their family's needs and most of their wants. Yet, in the back of their minds, they wonder what would happen if they were laid off, fired, or were injured and couldn't work. They keep this thought repressed because it breeds anxiety and fear. The house, the cars, the private schools, the club memberships, and several affiliations may need to be axed in order to stay afloat.

In the early 80's, my brother, Ralph, worked as an accountant for General Motors. When I would visit him in Flint, MI, life in the city was booming. The downtown area was teeming with festivals and concerts. The recession began in the mid 80's and the auto industry took a big hit. The plant started laying-off workers and the unions couldn't stop it.

People lost homes, cars, and many luxuries. Instead of the city booming, it was busted. Many dreams and hopes were shattered. Being in the Air Force shielded me from some of this anxiety. As long as I progressed and remained flexible, I could continue my career. However, I knew that the old axiom was true, "all good things must come to an end."

This time I decided that I would not take a "good job" but rather, I would take a job that I wanted. Money was not the main objective. Also, I didn't want a job to dictate where I would live and how long I would live there. It was time for me to take control of my future. I didn't want to end up in a well-paying job and then find out my job was being phased out or outsourced. There are several jobs that were thriving a few years ago and have now been eliminated. When were moved to Chattanooga, we saw that Volkswagen (VW) had begun building their first US plant. It seemed everyone was trying to get a job at

> *People lost homes, cars, and many luxuries.*

Volkswagen. If you got a job at VW it meant you were set and could live the good life.

I was fortunate to get a job in the VW Assessment Center. This is where candidates came to take a placement test for jobs in the plant. I saw people from all over the country come to take the assessment. Some of them were from the north and had experience working in the auto industry. One problem they faced was when they worked in the other plants, they didn't learn any computer skills. At least once a day I would hear, "I don't know much about computers." Without these updated skills, the candidate had little chance of being hired, even though they had years of experience. Always keep in mind that while technology increases productivity, it also decreases the number of producers needed.

Jobs come and go. If you are young and just starting an independent life, take the time to find your passion. In chapter 4, we talked about purpose. Your purpose provides provision. Please don't make the mistake of choosing a career based on salary. I talk to many young people who are attending college. At some time during the conversation I asked them about their major. Once they tell me their major, the next question is, "Why did you choose that major?" That's when I get the deer-in-the-headlights look or the shoulder shrug indicating IDK ("I don't know" for the technically challenged). There are a few that mention good pay. When playing dominoes, we have a saying, "All money ain't good money."

I can't count the number of times I was told not to let money rule me. In the early 70's I can remember being in Aunt Edith's living room and watching the olive colored 45 spinning on the console. Once the needle hit the record, the O'Jays gave us a message that many of us ignored:

"For a small piece of paper it carries a lot of weight
Call it lean, mean, mean green
Almighty dollar" (O'Jays)

Now to show you how rebellious and stubborn we were, we heard the O'Jays on Saturday, then on Sunday morning we turned our bibles to 1 Timothy 6:10 which reads:

"For the love of money is the root of all evil: which while some coveted after, they have erred from the faith, and pierced themselves through with many sorrows." (New Living Translation)

Can it be any plainer? Don't let money be the driving force on major decisions in your life. Take note the next time you're at a family gathering and listen to the number of people recalling the wasted time they spent chasing money and ended up catching a bag full of sorrows. Just know that you do not have to live this way. Chasing you passion is much more rewarding.

How would you like to get paid to do what you love? It is possible. Prior to making other life-long commitments such as marriage, children, and a "good job", try following your passion. Some people will tell you, "You can't make a living doing that." If you make them the subject of the statement, then it would be more accurate. The statement should be, "I can't make a living doing that." You can be successful at doing something you love even though it may be unconventional.

"Sand Masters" was a weekly television series. The storyline was about seven people who traveled the world building sand castles. Mind you, these were not the run-of-the-mill castles. The detail within these sculptures would stand up against works that use stone or ice. What's so amazing is that these people create structures that will be destroyed when the tide comes in. They worked in exotic places and met extraordinary people. (The Travel Channel) All of this while playing in the dirt; or at least it seems that way. These artists enjoy what they do and it shows in the works of art they create.

Here are a few well known people that made a pretty good living from following their passion:

- Winton Marsalis is passionate about music.
- Bill Gates is passionate about technology.
- Oprah Winfrey is passionate about communications.
- Sonia Sotomayor is passionate about law and justice.

When you are passionate about what you are doing, you don't settle for being good, you want to be great. You spend hours on end perfecting your craft. If you're going to be passionate it is paramount that you become the best you can possibly be.

For those who have already amassed numerous responsibilities that will not allow you to drop everything and follow your passion.

I challenge you to not give up on your dreams. This is easier said than done because some of our mistakes require that we make amends and endure the consequences. An example is found in the judicial system. Several young people have made mistakes and ended up in the penal system. After they've served their time, they may or may not be able to secure a job. In this case, they've made amends, yet the consequences of their actions continue to limit their opportunity to follow their passion.

In the case of bills, you must pay them. Some people have been mandated by law to pay a certain amount monthly. Those people will not be able to devote all of their time and energy to follow their passion. They have to first make sure they pay the money or end up behind bars. So what do you do? The solution is not easy. You are going to have to do double time. That may mean taking evening classes to get a certification. It may mean taking on-line classes to finish your degree. It may also mean that you have to work two or three menial jobs until you get a better one. The sacrifice will be painful, but the results will be the pleasure of doing what you love.

You can get paid to do what you love, and that love is within you. The question is, "Are you willing to do what it takes?" It is easier to just go with the flow by getting a good job and having the finer things in life. However, having the finer things won't fill the emptiness of not pursuing what you love. Look at it this way, would you want to be with the love of your life or would you want to be with someone who can give you a lot of the things you want? For me, there is no choice. I choose to look within me and follow my dreams.

Did You Hear What I Said?

1. Everything you need to be successful has already been placed in you.
2. Your passion can produce provision.
3. If you're passionate about something, you should strive to be the best at it.

Preparing the Next Generation

I was blessed to have parents, siblings, and extended family that provided me with the tools needed to cultivate the seeds God planted in me. Following their example, I want to give my children and others every opportunity to be successful. They need to be prepared for their future and not mine. In other words, they need to be equipped with updated tools. When I was in high school, I learned how to type on a manual typewriter.

Within four years I had to upgrade and learn how to operate an IBM Selectric.[21] At that time, an electric typewriter with a correction ribbon was cutting edge. Just when I mastered the Selectric, here comes the word processor. Instead of just typing, I had to also be proficient at function key operation. Continual updating was not an option for me, and it's definitely not an option for our children. They will need new tools to build their future.

School is one place that provides these tools. It is paramount that the next generation has the best education possible to ensure their future. We cannot waste time complaining about the public school system. Today, there are many educational options: home school, charter school, and private school, etc. These choices have wiped out all of our excuses. If we have children that are attending poor schools, we must get involved. We can't sit back and rely on someone to jump in and help. Our children are depending on us to do whatever it takes to get them where they need to be. That means if we need to turn off OUR favorite show in order to go to a parent-teacher conference or a school board meeting, then it's goodbye

---

[21] An electric typewriter introduced in the early 70's

television. It also means getting up when we're tired. Yes, we deserve a time of relaxation after a hard day at work. Shorten your relaxation time and then get up and make it happen for the children. Again, they are depending on us.

Our children can't afford to be behind. When I graduated in 1979, I didn't have to worry about competing with someone from another country when looking for work. We are living in a global economy and the world is getting smaller. When we call customer service, we have no idea who is on the other end of the call. They say that their name is John and their accent may be hard to understand. While we are sleeping, there are people in other countries that are up and at work. I am not advocating that America stops outsourcing jobs. Instead, I'm suggesting that we understand that this is the world we live in, adjust our way of thinking, and prepare for coming changes. When our children see that we are prepared for the future, hopefully, they follow our example.

Our children look to us as role models. In the area of finance, children take their cues from the parents. I must confess that I haven't always been Heathcliff Huxtable. There were many times (more than I want to admit), that financially I was more like Al Bundy. Although my children had everything they needed and most of what they wanted, I could have done a better job "showing" them how to let money work for them versus them working for money. Sometimes this is a hard fact to admit. No one enjoys acknowledging they were wrong. Once you've acknowledged a shortcoming, you can ask for forgiveness and move on. So how do you move on knowing that you've dropped the ball?

Start by getting your finances together. Once I was speaking to a group of people in a bible study. As I was speaking, I stopped and starred into the audience and told them that I had received a revelation. The audience was waiting to hear the rest. I said, "There is a word for everyone that wants to get out of debt." Someone in the audience shouted "Tell it!" In a low deliberate voice I said, "Pay your bills." Some were expecting some deep revelation of the Spirit. For them, that word was too simple. Their response was similar to Naaman's response to the prophet Elisha. In 2 Kings chapter 5, we are given an account of Naaman, the captain of the Syrian army. He was a powerful man, and he was a leper. He went to the prophet Elisha to be healed. Elisha sent a messenger to tell Naaman to go to the river

Jordan and dip seven times. Here is Naaman's response:

"Naaman went away angry. He said, Look, I thought for sure he would come out, stand there, invoke the name of the LORD his God, wave his hand over the area, and cure the skin disease." (New Living Translation)

The answer is simple; pay your bills. Next, let's get on a budget. I know; too simple. Keep in mind that we are the example for future generations. Budgeting ensures that we live within our means. The great thing about budgeting is that everyone can do it. You may say, "My paycheck fluctuates." That's fine, if you have that situation, then you can follow the bank's example. If you want a loan, they ask you to show your pay stubs for two months. They take that average of those pay stubs and use it as your "estimated income." Paying your bills and having a budget are crucial in coming out of the abyss of debt.

America has become a nation of debt. It has become normal to operate at a deficit. This mentality is not only at the federal level, it has also filtered down to the personal level. How many times have you heard, "You're going to always owe somebody?" There is some truth to this statement. More than likely you will at some point have to pay taxes and utility bills, and other. However, some of us have taken that statement to the nth degree.

At one point Laura and I had accumulated over $40,000 in credit card debt. This did not include regular bills such as car note, insurance, and education. We didn't have a lot of tangible things to show for it, but we've got some great pictures and great stories. Unfortunately, if you add $1 to the pictures and stories, you couldn't buy a decent cup of coffee. One day Laura and I decided to sit down with a financial advisor. He was very cordial and took time to look over our account. When he started asking us about each debt, the room temperature seemed to rise and it became very uncomfortable. The reason was because the advisor was exposing the real cause of our financial quagmire which was Wayne and Laura. After that session we were on our way to recovery.

> *We had over $40,000 in credit card debt*

Now our children and grandchildren have an example of making a mess of finances AND paying your debts. Thanks be to God that we learned from our experience and haven't made that mistake again. Since that we eliminated that debt, we have developed a low tolerance for excuses on why people don't pay their debts. In our travels we have met many people who make "good money", yet they are negligent in paying the money they owe. This is not very Christ-like. In fact, I would say that this type of behavior is rather wicked. Psalm 37:21 states:

"The wicked borrow and never repay; but the godly are generous givers." (New Living Translation)

To make things worse, this behavior is duplicated by the next generation. The children grow up thinking that you get whatever they want now, and they can pay for it when they get around to it. We've got to do better.

I stated earlier that I have not always been the best example for my children. Now that they are adults, I continually challenge them to do better. They must take the bad and not repeat it. They must take the good and duplicate it. Their children should have every opportunity they had and more. To help them with this goal, Laura and I have decided that we will plan for our grandchildren's future. One part of the plan is to buy them stocks.

While reading a biography on Warren Buffet, I found that his father bought him stocks when he was 11 years old. (WarrenBuffett) His father planted that seed and a few billion dollars later we see the fruit. At 8 years old, Serenity knows that she has stock in Nike™. Periodically, she comes to me and asks to check her stocks. This is usually after one of her friends brags about purchasing a new pair of Nike™ shoes. She understands that she doesn't have to be jealous, instead she can tell them, "Thank You."

Laura and I have also set up a college fund. If you haven't done this, do some research and get it done. When Ouidaintria graduated from high school in 2000, it was a time of celebration. Family from all over came to the graduation. Her grandfather Jack, wasn't able to attend, but he sent his gift to let her know how proud he was. When Ouidaintria told me about the gift I wasn't shocked. Jack had always been generous (The gift was a lot more than $20). Then I compared the money we had saved with the money Jack had given. Let's just say that on graduation day, Jack was the man. There was no college fund for our daughter. Time had passed and it was too late to start saving for college. Ouidaintria was starting school in less than 90 days. For those who've already put savings in place, good for you. For those who haven't, you might want to speed up. Your children will be graduating before you know it.

Our grandchildren's college fund come with prerequisites. A high school diploma is not the only requirement for accessing the money. Prior to graduation they will have to show us that they are mature enough to use the money to pursue their purpose. We are aware that everyone may not attend college after high school. However, they will not receive any funds to "find themselves". These funds will be released after a plan is developed. We understand that finance without purpose is waste, and we will help them make a life plan to pursue their purpose. I've often said that if one of the grandchildren decides that they don't want to comply with the prerequisites, Laura and I will take the money, purchase a vehicle, and get a personalized tag with the child's name on it.

Life has taught me that finance is not always complicated. I do not profess to be an expert, but I have made enough mistakes and had enough successes to be able to help others. It wasn't until Laura and I woke up, that we began to move forward. Teddy Pendergrass' voice penetrated the hearts of a generation with the following words:

"Wake up all the teachers, time to teach a new way
Maybe they'll listen to what you have to say
Cause they're the ones who are coming up and the world is in their hands
When you teach the children, teach them the very best you can" (Blue Notes)

These words still hold true today. We must teach our children to be financially savvy. They cannot make the same mistakes that we've made and expect the same results. If they repeat our mistakes, they will end up further behind. Let's catapult the next generation into their destiny. They can experience a life of more than enough and live in a way that we could only imagine. They also will be able to help their fellow brothers when the need arises. I believe it can happen and my prayer is that God will allow me to live to see it.

Did You Hear What I Said

1. Pay Your Bills!
2. Talk with a financial advisor.
3. Be an example of "what to do" and not an example of "what not to do."

WAYNE S. BROWN

Conclusion

It is my sincere hope that something in this book has inspired you to take action. You've probably already heard all of the main points in each chapter and that's a good thing. Repetition helps us remember. Below is a poem that I learned in grade school. Each time I read it, it reminds me of Momma's support and encouragement:

If you can't be a pine on the top of the hill,
be a scrub in the valley
But be the best little scrub by the side of the rill.
Be a bush if you can't be a tree.
If you can't be a bush, be a bit of the grass,
some highway happier make.
If you can't be a muskie, then just be a bass -
but the liveliest bass in the lake.
We can't all be captains; we've got to be crew.
There's something for all of us here,
There's big work to do, and there's lesser to do.
And the task we must do is near.
If you can't be a highway, then just be a trail.
If you can't be the sun, be a star.
It not by size that you win or you fail -
Be the best of whatever you are!
Douglas Malloch

The next time you're at a family gathering or reunion, take the time to listen to those who have your best interest in mind. They will give you invaluable wisdom that will take you further than you can imagine. If you happen to be that older person (like me) you have an obligation to share your stories. There will be those who will be too busy having a good time and there will also be those who will listen.

Peace

ABOUT THE AUTHOR

Wayne Brown is highly motivated with a passion for leading people towards their destiny. As an author, he uses humor and wit to tell stories that inspire others. As founder of Bridge-N-the-Gap, he seeks to pay it forward by mentoring youth and young adults. He is a 30 year veteran who has served in stations to include Europe, the Pacific, and the Middle East. He is active in the community, a ministry leader, and a devoted husband. He was born in Albany, GA and now lives in Chattanooga TN. Wayne and his wife Laura have three children and two grandchildren. For more information and booking, go to www.bridgenthegap.com or email Wayne at bridgenthegap@gmail.com

ABOUT THE COVER

The cover was designed by Laura Brown and Eric Finley, Jr. (artist) The scene takes place on the front porch of a home in Anytown USA. The men are talking about life and reminiscing while they watch the grandkids. The people in the scene are (from left to right): Wayne Brown (Pop-Pop), Justice (Grandson), Harmony (granddaughter), Serenity (granddaughter), and Irenus Brown Sr. (Big Pops). For more information about the artist Eric Finley, Jr., go to www.kingdom-graphica.com

Bibliography

BBC. 2014. Web. 22 06 2014.

Biography. 2014. Web. 22 06 2014.

Bluenotes, Harold Melvin and the. "Wake Up Everybody." *Chronology*. 1975. Album.

Brown, James. "Get Up Offa That Thing." Record, 1976.

Caesar, Shirley. "No Charge." *Ultimate Collection*. 1974. Album.

Control, Center For Disease. "National Diabetes Fact Sheet." 2011. Internet.

Earth, Wind, and Fire. "Boogie Wonderland." *I Am*. 1979. Album.

ESPN. 2014. eb. 19 6 2014.

Giese-Davis, Janine. *Journal of Behavioral Medicine* (2014): 22-36. Internet.

Heatwave. "Mind Blowing Decisions." *Central Heating*. 1978. Album.

Houghton, Israel. "I Know Who I Am." *A Deeper Level*. 2007. CD.

Ingredient, Main. "Everybody Plays the Fool." *Bitter Sweet*. 1972. Album.

Jackson, Michael. "Workin' Day and Night." *Off The Wall*. 1979. Album.

Johnston-Kohl, Laura. *People's Temple* Wayne Brown. 4
        2014. In Person.

"To A Mouse." MacLaclan, Robert Crawford and
        Christopher. *The Best Laid Schemes*. Princeton,
        NJ: Princeton University Press, 2009. 47-48.
        Book.

Merriam-Webster. 2014. Web. 19 6 2014.

Mission Readiness. 2014. Web. 20 6 2014.

NFL. 2014. Web. 21 6 2014.

O'Jays. "For the Love of Money." *Ship Ahoy*. 1973.
        Album.

"PBS." 2014. *PBS.com*. 2014.

Rucker, Darius. "This." *Charleston, SC 1966*. 2010. CD.

The Journal of Environmental and Public Health. 2014.
        Web. 19 06 2014.

The Travel Channel. 2014. Web. 22 06 2014.

US Constitution. 2014. web. 19 6 2014.

US Department of Health and Human Services. 2014.
        Web. 19 6 2014.

WarrenBuffett. 2014. Web. 22 06 2014.

Washington, Harriet. *Medical Apartheid*. New York:
        Doubleday, 2006. Book.

Made in the USA
Charleston, SC
28 July 2014